A Rebel's Religion

by Jess Hays

A Rebel's Religion

Copyright © 2014 by Jessica Hays
All rights reserved.
ISBN-10: 1503027104
ISBN-13: 978-1503027107

All Scripture quotations, unless otherwise indicated, are taken
from the New English Translation (NET).

All rights reserved. No part of this publication may be
reproduced, stored in a retrieval system, or transmitted in any
form by any means—electronic, mechanical, photocopy,
recording, or any other—except for brief quotations in printed
reviews, without the permission of the author.

Skull and cross design by Jevonne Ray

For more writings by Jess, visit her blog.

jess-hays.blogspot.com

Contact Jess at rebelsreligion@gmail.com

Table of Contents

For Dad, who taught me what it means to be a lifelong learner and who instilled in me curiosity and the confidence to pursue it.

Introduction

Wow! I cannot believe I am actually writing the introduction to my book. I'm not a writer, well not a real writer at least. I didn't go to school to be a journalist or to study creative writing. I didn't get a degree in literary eloquence nor do I do any form of writing for a living. In fact, most of my childhood, high school, and college years were spent in opposition to anything having remotely any connection to English class. Despite my dislike towards writing as an assignment and my inability to spell without the magic of auto correct, I have found some solace and comfort in the form of putting my feelings down on paper.

I'm not writing this book because my life is any more exciting or tragic than anyone else's. I'm writing it because I think we benefit from sharing one another's triumphs and struggles. Everyone has a unique journey, one that no one else can have. That's why sharing our stories are so important; it allows us to see God differently, to experience Jesus through one another.

This is my journey; some of my greatest failures, hardest battles, and most exciting triumphs. This is my journey of grace and how it changed my life in a deeper way than just saving my soul from hell. This is the story of how I gave up on religion and fell into a passionate love affair with Jesus. I hope my journey helps you along yours or at the very least, provides some interesting reading material for your rest stops.

1

Everyone Needs a Good Back Story

My journey begins with two people very much in love. From the moment I could process the feeling I knew my parents loved each other and, in turn, loved me. Dad was a youth pastor for most of my life, and we spent the early years of my childhood on the move bouncing from one Independent Baptist church to the next. There were always youth kids at our house playing games, having parties, and eating whatever delicious meal that mom made.

Just a few short months after being born I was being pushed along in my stroller at youth camp, as my mom and dad led their crazy band of students into the adventures of youth ministry. They were both so involved and so connected with their students.

Five years later my little brother was born, and we settled down as dad began his position as the youth pastor at a little church in Cedar Hill, Texas were my grandfather was the pastor. When we first moved to Cedar Hill, our family had about ten dollars to our name, but we were welcomed with open arms to live under the roof of my grandparents. Lack of money or a home of our own didn't stop dad from being intensely passionate about his place in that church, and our family jumped in head first as part of the congregation.

I was only six years old but it became my goal to stump and astound my Sunday School teachers with my vast knowledge of all things Biblical. Even from an early age I was extremely hardheaded, deeply passionate, and intensely determined. More times than not my parents were grabbed after the services and told stories of my fiery attitude and zealous heart, which was incredibly cute... as a toddler.

Time passed, I grew older, and both my parents took teaching jobs at a small Christian school in Ovilla, Texas that I also attended. The older I got, the more my passion wasn't as cute and got me in trouble as I became forcefully protective of the weak. One such time as this was my sixth grade Christmas party.

A boy in my class decided it would be fun to pick on and make fun of one of the girls. He called her names and took her candy off her plate. I'll never forget the pain in her eyes as silent tears slowly cascaded down her cheeks. Anger like a volcano welled up inside me and I grabbed the boy by the collar and pinned him up against the wall, demanding he leave her alone. He yelped for me to let him go with promises of retreat until the teacher came and peeled me off of him. I earned a stern talking to from my teacher, discipline from my parents, and a grateful smile from my bullied classmate.

Junior high years were hard. It became painfully obvious that I was different. I wore baggy clothes, shoes that were a couple of sizes too big, and my hair pulled tight into a bun. While other girls were going shopping, sharing make-up, and gossiping about boys, I spent every waking moment playing basketball and guitar. That's when I had to start protecting myself from the bullies instead of protecting others. Soon, I became the bully in anticipation that the ones I was bullying were going to hurt me.

Those years were riddled with fights, frustration, and a depth of pain that I hid inside myself. I wasn't the little girl I'm sure my mom wanted and because of the hard time I got at school any time she made a comment about my appearance it translated as yet another voice of disgust at who I was. I became more aware of how little time dad spent at home and how much he spent at work as his seat at my basketball games was consistently empty. This all laid the foundation for high school.

High school proved no easier than junior high was. More struggles came as my feelings of inadequacy were echoed by the voice of the church saying who I was wasn't enough there either. The more I looked for answers within Christianity the more I found a God who was more concerned with my performance within His religion than my desire for Him. I heard the message preached in chapel, accepted in churches, and taught in Bible class.

One specific moment is burned in my mind. I don't remember the exact topic we were discussing in class that day, but my Bible teacher took us to a verse in Matthew that states "be perfect as your heavenly father is perfect."[1] Then he took us over to a Hebrews passage where it's written, "the law made nothing perfect."[2] His conclusion was this: we should try to be perfect even though we never will be. Seriously? That's good news? That's what the disciples lived and died for? That's the message that Paul was willing to be tortured for? That our entire lives consist of us striving to be something that we will never achieve? I just couldn't do it anymore. What was the point in trying if I was never going to be enough?

So I gave up. I stopped trying to be what everyone expected of me. I discovered that alcohol made me numb, at least for a little while. Every bottle I poured down my throat buried my pain deeper and deeper, until I lost

---

[1] Matthew 5:48
[2] Hebrews 7:19

myself. I didn't have control anymore and I couldn't function without some kind of alcohol running through my veins. At one point it got so bad I would wake up in the morning from the two hours of sleep I managed to force myself into, brush my teeth, and make myself a nutritious breakfast of cereal and beer.

Most of my first year of college is a blur. Work and school became my new numbing agent as I filled my days with twenty-one hours worth of classes and forty five hour work weeks. I didn't sleep. I just worked and went to school and played music until I finally passed out around four or five in the morning. I had little desire for God and though I did visit churches of different denominations, values, and cultures it seemed the only thing they could agree on was that who I was wasn't enough for God.

I've had many people ask me what made me change, what made me look for something different. I'm never too sure how to answer that question. I'm not sure if it was even one specific moment or thing that sparked a desire to change. I just knew that something different needed to happen.

It wasn't some mystical experience like you hear about in church where God comes down and shows me all the things I need to change and I miraculously become a super Christian. Was that too cynical? For some people

14

that may be the case but for me it wasn't. My experience was one of complete brokenness. I became painfully aware of my life crumbling away without any ability to stop it. The more aware of this I became, the more I came to the realization that I felt completely empty inside. This was followed by the realization that what I was trying to use to feel whole wasn't working and I needed help outside of myself.

Thus began a new stretch in my journey as I took off in pursuit of something that could sweeten my bitterness, patch up my tattered heart, and fill the depth of my emptiness. A journey that started, not on the steps of a church, but in an empty classroom that was home to my first AA meeting.

2

The Road to Recovery

17

The room shined with the annoying brightness of those energy saving florescent bulbs that saved the planet while simultaneously giving me a migraine. The smell of packaged cookies and strong coffee filled the air and the hum of tired voices bounced off the walls. My eyes darted back and forth nervously as I still tried to decide whether or not I should really be here.

A loud, deep voice called us to sit down in a circle and I spun around to see its origin. That was when I saw Bob. He was a tall muscular man, covered in tattoos, with a five o'clock shadow that looked like it was there on purpose. He wore the same outfit every week, black scuffed combat boots, baggy black jeans complete with chain wallet, and a grey tank top that was most of the time covered in grease stains. Despite his rough appearance, he had kind eyes and an encouraging smile that eased some of my nervousness at being there.

He was the leader of this rag tag group of broken people and it seemed everyone looked at him with awe and respect as he began the meeting.

Long ago I had thought that ending up in a place like this, with people like this, meant I was a failure. That if I couldn't achieve healing with simple prayer and dedication to God, I wasn't good enough. I felt so alone, so broken, so utterly incapable of fixing myself. I didn't care anymore if being in this place made me a failure; in my mind that's exactly what I was and that was exactly where I needed to be. So, there I was, sitting in that circle, because I definitely wasn't good enough on my own.

One by one they all went around introducing themselves with "Hello, my name is _____, and I'm an alcoholic." Followed by the chorus of voices responding with, "Hello, _____." I chuckled at the adherence to the stereotype I saw repetitively in the movies. I don't know if anyone used their real names; I know some didn't and I was among them, but still that fleeting moment when someone was brave enough to name their addiction... it felt more authentic than I had experienced in a very, very long time.

Then, suddenly, the room fell silent and I looked up to see a room full of eyes on me. A tickle of panic moved in my stomach until I felt a strong but gentle hand on my shoulder as Bob said, "It's ok, it's just your turn." I gave out a sigh of relief accompanied by a half-hearted grin at my silliness. I then managed to stutter out "Umm, I'mm-m J-J-Jay, and uhhh, I'm an alcoholic." That was the first time I had actually admitted it out loud. Everyone clapped, those seated close hugged me, and Bob gave me a reassuring nod saying, "Welcome to the party!"

Bob appointed himself my sponsor, even though he didn't really do that anymore. Later he told me it was because he saw depth in my eyes and those were his favorite kinds of people. Whatever the reason, I was happy, he was kind and even when he told me hard truths he did it with love in his eyes and a strong arm around me, shoulder ready for tears. He was very black and white, very matter of fact, and very real. He cursed like a sailor and knew the Bible like the back of his hand (which incidentally had "rebel" carved across it). All of which made me love him all the more.

We would have long talks over coffee that were filled with authenticity and laughter. I had never felt so free to be me. He loved to play something he called "The Question Game." We took turns asking each other questions and no matter what it was you had to answer it honestly. I still use that game today when I want to get to know new people. That was how we learned one another's stories.

He told me about growing up in foster care with a mother greedy for government money and a father who beat them in his drunken rages. When he was 12 he escaped the abusive house he still refuses to call a home and took on life in the streets. By 14, he was a full-fledged gang member who had already robbed a bank and been shot. He finally ended up in prison where a good chaplin introduced him to Jesus and Bob started a new life. When he got out of prison he was determined to make a new way for himself. Where he had found good feelings in the bottom of whiskey bottles, he now found in helping other people. Now, he uses his street knowledge to reach out to forgotten and broken people like him who need desperately to be loved.

I admired him.

He made me feel guilty for hurting so much over so little.

One day I finally found the courage to admit this to him. He responded with, "Ha, I felt the same way about you. I would much rather have a screwed up relationship with people than a screwed up relationship with God. I mean, hell, you get pain from the one thing that keeps me going." I never really saw it that way, maybe because I was so plagued with guilt for simply being imperfect.

Despite my great coffee meetings with Bob and my increasing boldness in my AA meetings, my nights were still filled with sleeplessness. I began to think there was something physically wrong with me. These thoughts were reinforced by, what I now know to be, panic attacks. At first, I thought it was part of my withdraws from alcohol, just another addition to the cold sweats and shakes that came from forcing my body to let go of the addiction. Soon though, the latter two faded away and my panic attacks persisted.

I reluctantly made myself a doctor's appointment, completely sure I was going to be charged twenty five dollars just to get a lecture about the dangers of drinking. The doctor asked me a plethora of questions, scribbling in his notebook whenever I said something seemingly interesting. He took some blood and handed me a magazine as he went off to run some tests.

I laid back on the exam table, trying desperately to quiet the voices of worry that were screaming in my mind. I was so exhausted. The click of the door opening as the doctor came back in the room startled me. Finally, He was ready to give me a diagnosis. His words rang in my ears.

"You're suffering from depression."

He had the suffering part right but depression? The word added another weight to tip the scales of failure in my direction. He went on to explain how my hormones were imbalanced and that to help them balance out I would need to take some anti-depressants for a while. He also advised I see a therapist to help me know how to cope with my anxiety.

We don't talk about depression within the church and when we do it's with levity and insignificance. Depression is seen as just a symptom of sin or a disease that can be easily fixed by prayer and a healthy amount of Bible study. I've even been told that if you're a Christian then you can't have depression because depression is a demon not a sickness. What a devastating lie to tell people; what a hope shattering statement to be told.

Are we really so dense within the church that we think we can never get upset, sad, unhappy, or hurt after we accept Christ? Isn't that a little unrealistic? Besides, how does that make those people who live in the real world feel when those emotions happen? I'll tell you, we feel like shit. Hey, if you want honesty, there's not a better word for that feeling. It's even worse for those like us who have no control over the fact that our bodies have screwed up hormones, which I'm pretty positive, has nothing to do with whether or not Jesus loves me. Then again, maybe they just left that part out of the song.

I still wasn't sure if I was a failure or my religion was. Whatever the case, I was already going to AA so I might as well start going to therapy, right? I mean, I always was one to do it big. So, I began seeing a free counselor with my school. I was, after all, a poor student and I definitely wanted nothing to do with the Christian counseling found within the churches around the area.

3

How Do You Feel About That?

Doc was a feisty woman with short spikey hair, a quick tongue, and a laugh that made you feel more like you were at a bar than in the office of a shrink. She instantly put me at ease and filled the entire first session with meaningless questions about my favorite drink, candy, and music. All of these she had ready and set out for me at my next session which made me feel important even if I had lost my marbles.

She was a Christian but she didn't medicate me with Bible verses and prayers; in fact, she didn't mention God unless I did, which was rare. It still took me a while to open up, but eventually I did and we began to dive into the root of my issues. I had a journal that was given to me as a graduation present from a friend and she encouraged me to start writing again. Three months into our visits, I slept for eight hours straight.

It felt like an instant the way time passed and it was soon approaching my one year sobriety mark. The shakes were finally completely gone and I could at least hear the word beer without wanting to run to the nearest liquor store. A new struggle began to present itself in the form of facing the junk that drove me to that place. It was a scary place to be for me. The whole point in drinking was so that I didn't have to deal with the junk.

She was patient, and calm, and let me be real. Every day, she would just listen, sometimes asking questions that I didn't have an answer to and would send me home determined to have an answer for her the next day. Every day, from day one, when I walked out the door she would put her hand on my shoulder, look in my eyes, and say "I love you, Jess." Every day my response was the same, "Umm... you don't even know me!"

Then that day came, a year into being sober, I plopped down into my favorite chair in her office and popped the top on my diet coke. I barely had time to get my first sip down when she just came out with, "Why do you hate God, Jess?" I'm almost positive I came close to spewing my coke all over her. "I don't hate God... I just... I'm never going to be enough for Him... I'm pretty sure He hates me." She shook her head the way she did when I would curse at the stupidity of boys and declare my decision to become a nun. "Is that why you act so tough all the time? Because you think if God hates you everyone must?" I shrugged my shoulders, "I don't know. I guess so."

I tried to change the subject but she was just as stubborn as me and she pushed deeper. "I know you don't like church, why is that?" That one I was more than happy to answer (I am going to censor this one for the conservatives in the audience). "Church. Ha! Because all church is a bunch of hypocritical jerks who care more about how long your skirt is than if you actually want to know about God. It's so freaking stupid. All they do is just tell you over and over again how worthless God thinks you are while pretending to be perfect. At the same time, their own families are falling apart. How can someone want that? I don't meet the requirements of being a "good" Christian and I'm glad because I don't want to be anything like those people. I mean, I'm saved, but I don't know if that's even enough anymore."

I remember this like it was yesterday, every word, and I remember looking up at her when I finished my spew of anger to see sadness in her eyes. I felt bad about what I said for the first time in a long time. "I'm sorry... I didn't mean to hurt your feelings... I know you're not like that." She smiled but her eyebrows still furoughed in sadness. "Jess, I am truly sorry for those people who hurt you, who told you that you weren't enough and made you think that God hates you. Jesus is enough. You are enough. God loves you for all that you are, in your brokenness and anger and hurt. Embrace that and you will find peace like you've never known."

That's when I realized the sadness in her eyes was for me and I cried. I hadn't cried like that in a long time. I was too hardened by my hurt to cry anymore. Those words somehow found their way to the one soft spot left in my heart.

She pulled out her Bible for the first time since we'd been meeting and showed me what is now my favorite Bible verse, "Now the Lord is the Spirit and where the Spirit of the Lord is there is freedom."[3] I'd seen it before but this time it meant something different. I desperately wanted freedom, I craved peace, I was tired of having to be hard and tough constantly.

I left there that day with puffy eyes and plenty to think about. I didn't know then but that would be my first step on a long road that led me to the power of grace. As I walked out, just like every other day and with the exact same look as the ones preceding it, she looked in my eyes and said, "I love you, Jess." This time I found myself wrapping her up in a hug and whispering, "I love you too."

I didn't sleep at all that night, but the next session I walked into her office more invigorated than I ever had been. We talked for the rest of the week about finding peace in my life, not just with God but with my family, my friendships, and my job. I started to see that the more I

---

[3] 2 Corinthians 3:17

found peace with God the better I was at bringing peace to the other relationships in my life. Which makes sense to me now looking back because you can't give something out that you haven't received.

That weekend I wrote this in my journal:

Finding Passivity

Peace finding presence in passiveness

So long hidden by aggressive fists

Suffocated by bitterness

Built up and driven by a hit list

Never has been felt such relief

Like a fire extinguished to save what's underneath

Once clenched tight now released

Allowing reality to finally be seen

She didn't know what she was starting when she asked me that first question that day. On second thought, maybe she did. Grace and peace, they have the power to transform a person. Church, religion, and duty all fall short in that area. Restraint cannot change actions any more than a strait jacket can heal a sick mind.

That day she introduced me to a new idea. The idea that Jesus didn't die to save us only from our sins but from our bondage, our depression, and our gaping holes of emptiness that keep us up at night and corrode our souls. He died to free us from the captivity of our addictions and our religion, of our shattered lives and our plastic faces, of our evil and our efforts which are sometimes the same thing.

This was a new idea of Jesus that I had never heard before, one that made me want to purse getting to know Him better. That day she gave me a God to pursue and I took off full speed after Him.

Will The Real Jesus Please Stand Up?

My first hurdle to jump was trying to figure out who the real Jesus was. I would guess that you may be asking, "Isn't there only one Jesus?" Naturally, you would think finding out who the real Jesus is wouldn't be that difficult, but I've seen many Jesuses.

First, we have Protesting Jesus. This Jesus is at the front of the picket line, the hurler of insults at gay pride events, and the master of disdainful looks outside abortion clinics. Many people preach in the name of this Jesus, calling us to action against the masses of sinful humans roaming our streets and invading our schools.

Closely related to him, is Political Jesus. He is involved in making sure the right president from the right political party gets elected. If somehow he fails at this job, this Jesus is the one who gives you the go ahead to hate the president elected instead. He is also the one who advocates an aggressive and hateful push for teacher led prayer in schools and the requirement of the hanging of the Ten Commandments in our courtrooms.

Then there is Emotionally Demanding Jesus, who demands all of our love, affection, devotion, and desire, forbidding us to give any to anyone or anything else. If we withhold any of these things from him he is filled with jealousy and withholds his blessing as well as puts our relationship with him at odds. To me this Jesus sounds like a grumpy toddler.

Checked Out Jesus makes his debut next. If I follow this Jesus I had better make sure I'm doing my duties and forgiving seventy times seven times because if not, he won't be able to hear my prayers. Bad followers depress him and drain him of his affection so this Jesus checks out and leaves us to figure things out on our own.

Oh, and how could I forget Break-up Jesus? Come on, every teenager who has ever been in a youth group knows this Jesus. He's the one that tells your Christian girlfriend/boyfriend to break up with you because he wants them to "kiss dating goodbye." He's also the one who gives the "OK" for Christian marriages to end if they aren't "equally yoked."

None of these Jesuses sound too appealing which is why I didn't want anything to do with Him for so long. Then I found a new Jesus, the real Jesus. Surprisingly it was in the midst of turmoil in my life. I laugh, even now while I write this, at how frustratingly great God is sometimes.

Things went well for a while as I took large strides in the healing process. Soon though, I was presented with new challenges and tests on my sobriety. It seemed everything started to go bad at once. My job was, to say the least, difficult thanks to a boss who spent more time on his computer than doing his job which left people like me to pick up the slack. My friends who were more like family were getting a divorce and I had somehow found myself in the middle of it. I had a falling out with my pastor back home who was one of the few people I actually trusted. I was three hours away from home; I had no desire to be there and I had no desire to be where I was.

I started to consider drinking again as the feelings of inadequacy lay heavy on my heart. I had nowhere to run and no one to lean on; I felt hopeless. I buried myself in work, which wasn't hard because it was basketball season and I spent most of my waking hours bandaging up the girls' basketball team. There I was, typical Jess, healing everyone else's hurts while simultaneously ignoring my own.

Meeting Zorro was no exception to that rule.

I'm not sure why I reached out to him when I felt nothing but anger towards men as a whole. The ones I had trusted destroyed me and I had no room in my heart for another betrayal. Still, as I said before, I was busy healing everyone else but myself, and I saw hurt in his eyes. Our first real conversation consisted of me griping at him for throwing himself a pity party fueled by his bitterness. I'm surprised he talked to me after that. Later he told me I couldn't get rid of him that easily. I'm glad I didn't.

Our friendship grew and I helped him through some of the hard times that came his way with the full intention of fixing him and ditching him. I had no desire to get close. That plan backfired. I still don't know how, but he saw straight through me, he saw the depth of my pain behind my goofy smile and sarcastic toughness. That must have been when he decided I wasn't going to get rid of him.

He had a fight on his hands, that's for sure, as I put him through test after test to prove his loyalty and asked him over and over again what he wanted from me. With every doubtful demand he answered, "I don't want anything, J; I just wanna love ya!" I couldn't believe that. Still, he didn't give up, though I'm sure I made him want to at times. Soon, after a breakdown and a break through, he gained my complete trust. I'm pretty sure he still doesn't know how big of an accomplishment that is.

From then on we were a team. We raised hell and faced hell together. We leaned on each other and even if we were both falling apart we were trying to hold the other one together. He gave me courage to face demons from my past and reconcile with my family. Things I never thought I would ever be able to do. To this day I still consider him someone whose counsel and friendship I value.

He constantly amazed me with his ability to show love and grace to the people trying to destroy him. He sacrificed every day for the betterment of his kids, his family, his job, and his friendships. The more I think about the kind of man he is, the more I am in awe of how far along he is on a journey he has never even heard preached to him. He just knows God loves him and he relates out of that fact.

That is Jesus. The real Jesus.

Jesus finds us when we aren't even looking for Him. He embraces us when we tense up at the thought of affection. Jesus is patient in our doubt. In our statements of our worthlessness and our questioning of His requirements He answers, "I don't want anything, I just want to love you." Jesus gives grace even to those who are determined to destroy Him. He sacrificed all He had, holding back nothing, so that we could have everything.[4] That's my Jesus.

Meeting this Jesus, the real Jesus, made me want to learn everything I could about Him. It caused me to reexamine my faith (or lack thereof) and rethink how He related to me. Jesus made my faith intimate and authentic and more than just the cold hard fact that religion had offered me for so long. Jesus called me out from under my steeple to run recklessly with him through the grunge of life, jumping in mud puddles along the way, and rolling around delightfully in the dust of my rabbi.

---

[4] Philippians 2:5-8

5
Faith of Demons

Spending my life teething on pews and getting my education from a Christian school caused the Bible and even Christianity to become very academic to me. When I say that I mean that my Bible became more of a text book to me than a guide to life, so to speak; I reduced God to simply another subject in my assignment folder.

I am very analytical by nature; I tend to be a very task and fact driven person. This made putting God in the academic box easy for me. I became really interested in Apologetics (defending your faith). The basic idea behind Apologetics is having the ability to defend your faith against any argument that you may ever encounter from any non-Christian or skeptic of any type.

I went to Apologetics camps, read countless books covering it, and even wrote articles about it in my school newspaper. I had pretty much all the head knowledge possible when it came to defending my faith. It helped me function, at first. I was the kid that always questioned everything, pushed the lines, and challenged the norm and learning Apologetics allowed me to question and test everything that I was taught to believe in and determine if it were true without being told that my questioning meant I was doubting God, which was the most unpardonable of sins.

There was a problem though; it was all just head knowledge. I knew every rational argument to prove Christianity, I knew every Bible verse reference to back up my beliefs, I even knew all the biblical history behind every story, but it didn't change my life. I was really still just a skeptic living under the guise that I had the answers.

All that knowledge didn't keep me from becoming an alcoholic or getting in fights or hanging with the wrong people. It didn't heal the deep scars on my heart from having my trust betrayed. It didn't drive the bitterness inside me away or comfort my loneliness. All that knowledge didn't help me at all.

James wrote, "You believe that there is one God. Good! Even the demons believe that—and shudder."[5] I believed in God, that He was real, that His son died to save me, and I feared Him. I feared punishment, feared judgment, and feared disappointing Him. I lived my life cowering in the corners of my own inadequacy because I

---

[5] James 2:19

really believed, in the depths of who I was, that God was upset with me.

All the things that I did, the services I attended, the sacrifices I made, even my obsession with gaining knowledge about this religion we name after Christ, I did it all because I was devastatingly terrified of God's wrath. I had a faith of demons and I needed something radically different.

It took me a long time to discover who Jesus really was, but when I did it quickly changed who I was. Only then did I feel free to stop worrying about being enough because I knew I was loved even if I wasn't enough. I became slower to anger and I regained my soft heart. I found it easier to forgive those who hurt me within my family and church and determined to be a pursuer of peace. I embraced honesty as I decided being real with people was more important than being impervious. I made amends with my parents and revealed to them my alcohol addiction which I had kept hidden for so long. They cried.

I worry that, in that moment, they felt like failures as parents. They shouldn't feel that way. They didn't fail me. I was looking for something they could never give me, and I should never expect them to. I felt like I let them down because I didn't turn out to be the daughter they deserved. They never saw me that way though, not really. They loved me and embraced me. My little brother still looked up to me and my dad still told me he was proud of me, though I in no way deserved it. Grace shone brightly that night as we laid new bricks of trust for a foundation of peace within our home.

A little over a year after that, I managed to graduate from college and, much to my chagrin, had to move back in with my parents. I was worried at first that things would return to the way they were when I was in high school. My worries proved to be pointless; after all, I was very different now and so were they. I remembered that night the year before when they embraced me in my messiness and showered me with love, and I was confident that this place would now be a safe place to run to, a safe place from the storms of life.

Transitioning was still difficult as I went from having my own apartment, making my own rules, and having my own space to sharing space and time with three other people. Even so, I treasured being around my family again and being able to lavish them with love, something I never had the ability to do in the past because I had no love in my heart to pour out. We grew together and I soon returned to our church.

I was a little gun shy jumping back in as I found that there were some hurts still associated with that place. I found it hard to trust certain leaders within the church as glimmers of my past flashed before me. Soon my doubts were settled.

Upon returning, I discovered that the atmosphere was different than when I left, it was more authentic, more filled with love, and more inviting. I don't know if that was because I had changed so much or they had; whatever the case, I felt peace there. As soon as I started hearing the messages every Saturday night I was completely won over as my pastor described an extreme of grace I had never imagined.

Encounter is a different kind of church. We meet on Saturday nights instead of Sundays (No, we are not Seventh Day Adventists). We have a band and a drum set instead of an organ and a choir. Our pastor wears jeans, uses an iPad instead of a printed Bible, and speaks behind a music stand instead of a pulpit. The people greet you with hugs and good coffee even when they don't know you that well. Our chairs are filled with religion junkies, strippers, former drug addicts, divorcees, rebels turned into revolutionaries, and tattooed recovering alcoholics like me.

I had some struggle with understanding grace at first. For so long I was such a lover of justice, and in some ways I still am. It was hard for me to reconcile the God of extreme justice and the God of extreme grace. I didn't think they could coexist. It required me to completely retrain my mind and expand my thinking. That's when I discovered the justice of grace.

6

Grace and Justice

First I should explain what I mean when I talk about grace. The word grace gets tossed around a lot in the church so I have found that when I sit down and talk about grace with other Christians we aren't always on the same page.

I've heard quite a few definitions of grace, but the two most well-known within the church are the following:

G.R.A.C.E = **G**od's **R**iches **A**t **C**hrist's **E**xpense (please imagine that being said it my best snotty little girl voice).

Grace = The getting of what we don't deserve.

Technically, both are true about grace but I'm not sure if I would define grace by them. Grace is more than just a memorized definition we teach our children in Sunday school. It is bigger than just getting something we don't deserve. In his book, *The Ragamuffin Gospel,* Brennan Manning writes, "Grace is the active expression of God's love for us."[6] What a beautiful truth! How gloriously scandalous of a perfect Divinity to choose as His expression of love such a one way avenue. Grace is the complete and total favor of God, in fullness, right now, even when we sin. This takes grace to an extreme where I, at first, found it hard to see God's justice fit in.

I'm a lover of justice. I like for good people to get rewarded and bad people to be punished. Around age seven, I set my heart on being a police officer when I grew up. I would dress up every year for Halloween as a police officer and my biggest hero on the planet was my uncle who was, you guessed it, a police officer. As I grew up, my view of the world grew darker and I lost my naivety. I realized that being in a profession driven by law wasn't so glamorous.

Part of what made me so cynical toward religion was all the injustice I saw happening around me. People who claimed righteousness but lived hypocritically were rewarded for fooling everyone around them. Not me... I saw them for what they were.

People like that taught me how to be hard, how to hate fake religion, how to fear failure and hide heartache. Growing up around those kinds of people made me crave justice. The more I experienced and was shown grace,

---

[6] The Ragamuffin Gospel, Brennan Manning, Pg. 39

which I desperately needed, the more confused I became. I found grace to be so irresistible that I caught myself running full speed after it down an unknown road without any desire to look back. This caused a war to rage inside me between my head that said I deserved punishment for my enormous amount of life failures, and my heart that said God's grace has declared me freed and forgiven.

So, I did what I do best, I researched. I read as many books as I could get my hands on that covered this idea of radical grace. I spent hours talking to anyone who would sit down with me and allow me to doubt and be argumentative and question everything I thought I knew about God. I drank large amounts of coffee, tattered the pages of my Bible, and covered the pages of my journal with rainbow colored glimpses at God.

After all that, after months and months of study, the conclusion I came to is this: We have a choice. We can choose to live by the "do to get" system where the harder we work the more we get. In this system we have to keep the entirety of the law to be right with God, basically live perfect lives. It's a system so common in our world and so completely impossible to live up to that we end up feeling like a failure, which we constantly are within that system.

On the other hand, we can choose to take in the totality of grace given to us by Jesus's death on the cross. A grace that declares us absolutely clean and free from all failures past, present, or future. A grace that keeps and satisfies the entire law for us. A grace that doesn't just overlook our failures but actually makes us into successes.

Whichever system we choose is the one we will be judged by, that's God's complete justice. The choice is grace and the judgment is justice.

For a justice lover like me it made perfect sense, and it made me love grace even more. I became filled with the desire to learn about anything and everything that had to do with grace. I wanted it in extremes and I didn't care if it broke all the rules about balance within the church. It was in this pursuit that I discovered how wonderfully messy life with Christ is.

7

Dust of the Rabbi

In the Jewish culture of Jesus's time, people related to one another based on a cultural social scale. The higher up you were on that social scale the more respect and honor you were given by others. Their lives were built around this system; their identities tied to it.

Their religion was an integral part of this system. Young boys began their education of this religion as early as age six by the end of which they would have the entire Torrah (first 5 books of the Bible) memorized. At the end of that time, those who didn't make the cut would be sent back home to their families to learn the family trade, while the best students would continue on in their education and memorize the rest of the Law and the Prophets. That's the entire Old Testament... memorized. The best of those bests would then find a Rabbi, a teacher of the Law, someone given great honor and respect, and these bests would go to that Rabbi and ask to be his talmid, his disciple.

The rabbi would sit him down and ask him question after question about scripture and Jewish traditions and laws, testing him to see if he was worthy of being his talmid. This could go on for hours, a rigorous test, to decide if this boy was worthy of the rabbi. Then, at the end of it, if the rabbi thought this kid was cut out to be part of his pack he would say to the boy, "Come, follow me." This calling was one of the highest honors and a difficult one to obtain, and it was only given to the best of the best of the best.

Jesus comes on the scene and changes things. We find Jesus beginning his rabbi career walking on the beach calling out to some fishermen. Fishermen, low on the social scale, dirty, uneducated, fishermen. Not the best of the best. Fishermen with unkempt beards that stank of salt air and fish scales, and Jesus calls to them, "Come, follow me."

What Jesus is saying here is not just, "Hey let's be best friends and go travel the world and stuff." This is a higher call, this is the greatest of honors, a rabbi calling to fishermen, "Come, be my disciples."

No wonder they left all they had ever known, all they had ever done, their father sitting in the boat, to run off after Jesus. This was the opportunity of a lifetime, one they had been labeled as not good enough for in the past.

I think sometimes we get this idea that discipleship is really only for the elite of the faith, like the ones who have studied hard and have it figured out, the ones who go to the rabbi and ask to be one of his disciples. I sometimes think this way. I think to myself, maybe if I study a little bit more, if I have the answers to most of the questions, then maybe I will deserve the title of disciple.

We get this idea in our heads that God wants us to measure up first, to clean up first before we can be called His. Which, if you think about it, is really ridiculous because Jesus spent most of His time on this earth hanging with the dirty, the socially awkward, and the not good enough. Not only that, but he leaves His message in the hands of these uneducated, not good enough to be disciples, fishermen and tells them to go build his church, to go be who He was, to go love like He loved. Surely, Jesus could have found men much more qualified for such a calling?

But He didn't.

He called those men, the underqualified riff-raff. He didn't even wait for them to come beg to be His. He went out and found them in the midst of their not enough and he called them to be His.

Think about the circumstances of your call, brothers and sisters. Not many were wise by human standards, not many were powerful, and not many were born to a privileged position. But God chose what the world thinks foolish to shame the wise, and God chose what the world thinks weak to shame the strong. God chose what is low and despised in the world, what is regarded as nothing, to set aside what is regarded as something, so that no one can boast in his presence."[7]

They had this beautiful saying in Jewish culture, a blessing that they would say to disciples. They would say, "May you be covered in the dust of your rabbi." The goal of a disciple was to do everything like the rabbi, to be like the rabbi. The idea behind this blessing is that you would follow so close by behind your rabbi that by the end of the day you would be covered in whatever gunk and grime he had stepped in along the way. You would be caked in the very dust from his feet and it would be a blessing. It's impossible to live a life in pursuit of Jesus and not be covered in His dust.

Our problem is we think that we need to clean ourselves up, and in the process we scrub off the dust of our rabbi, by the end of which we look nothing like Him anymore. God, He's a God of the mess. He bends down and squishes mud between His fingers and then uses it to do miracles. He kisses dust and creates life. He calls us to

---

[7] 1 Corinthians 1:26-29 (NET)

a life of messy adventure, a life outside the social scale, a life covered in the dust of the rabbi.

God is a different kind of God and Jesus a different kind of rabbi; this I was learning quickly. How wonderfully refreshing to know that God is vastly different than I had thought Him to be for so long. This knowledge completely changed how I saw Him. Still, I wrestled with another question: How does God see me exactly?

I wasn't really sure. All I knew for sure is how I deserved to be seen. God didn't seem to be any better at following the rules than I was so maybe he saw me differently than I deserved. I tried not to think about it much, scared that the answer might destroy the peace I so happily clung too.

The longer I procrastinated in finding the answer the more it affected my relationship with other people. This taught me a valuable lesson; how I perceive that God relates to me will be how I relate to other people. I finally gave in and decided to go in search of how God saw me.

My initial thoughts were reminiscent of an old song I sang when I was a child called "God's Still Workin' on Me." It goes like this:

There really ought to be a sign upon my heart

Don't judge him yet, there's an unfinished part

But I'll be better just according to His plan

Fashioned by the Master's loving hands

He's still working on me

To make me what I need to be

It took him just a week to make the moon and stars

The sun and the earth and Jupiter and Mars

How loving and patient He must be

'Cause He's still workin' on me[8]

It sounds really great, encouraging even. For some time I found hope in the fact that God hasn't given up on me and he's still working to make me better. I often thought of myself as a work in progress. I was comforted in thinking that even though I wasn't perfect yet; I was better than I used to be.

---

[8] Heavenly Highway Hymnal

Perfection is a scary concept. So many negative connotations accompany it that it brings with it an oppressive cloud of inadequacy. Our world offers us many definitions of, roads to, and pictures of perfection; each one convincing us that we are just aren't quite hitting the mark. Then begins our desperate attempts to convince ourselves that it's ok if we don't.

"Nobody is perfect!" we say.

We hear about perfection in the church too. It's spoken of as a far off state of being that we will reach "someday" and that's ok with us. It keeps us hopeful as it sparkles dimly in the distance encouraging us of how great we might be after death. Still we strive for it. We stack up our accomplishments, our great godly deeds, and think to ourselves "Look how good I am!" Then we fail. We hide it, brushing it under the rug, pretending that it's okay.

"Nobody is perfect!" we say.

Two different worlds telling us the same lie. The lie that we can never be perfect and to never stop trying. The lie that leaves us hearing nothing but the voice that screams, "You will never be good enough!"

How sly Satan is in the lies he tells us. Whispering into our logic, sneaking into our religion, slowly convincing us that we are still broken, and in need of road work signs strewn along our lives. So often we expect him to work within the overtly evil things that we miss him crawling through our pews, singing through our hymns, and working through our Christian duties.

The truth is… You are perfect. Right here, right now, in this moment while you read this, you are perfect.

All those years ago when Christ, the perfect man, willingly walked to His death; sin was defeated. Death was conquered. The power of the law to condemn us was stripped away and His perfection was offered to us, the dirty and broken. When we accept that, when we take in that free gift that is offered to us who don't deserve it, our spirits become one with His.[9] Everything thing He has, the essence of Him, yes, even His perfection becomes ours!

John writes that we may have confidence on the day of judgment, "…because just as Jesus is, so are we in this world."[10] We are perfect because He is perfect! Our status of perfection then becomes based on how perfect He remains before the Father. We have no ability to be any more or less perfect that we already are! As Jesus is,

---

[9] 1 Corinthians 6:17
[10] 1 John 4:17b (NET)

so also are we! You can stop trying your best to be "good enough" for Him, for others, or even for yourself. What an encouraging truth to discover! It was further assured in my mind after finding a wonderful verse in Philippians:

> "Therefore let those of us who are perfect embrace this point of view. If you think otherwise, God will reveal to you the error of your ways. Nevertheless, let us live up to the standard that we have already attained."
>
> ~Philippians 3:15-16~

The more I looked the more I saw God's grace and the less I saw God's demands. In fact, the actions that I thought defined being a Christian were actually only a result of taking in grace.

Understanding that God saw me as completely righteous still proved difficult as I had to unlearn what I had been taught for so long. I spent a lot of time wresting with such a radically new idea and eventually took to drawing myself a picture that helped me bridge the gap between my old way of thinking and the truth. Lucky you, I have included it on the next page just so you can admire my amazing art skills!

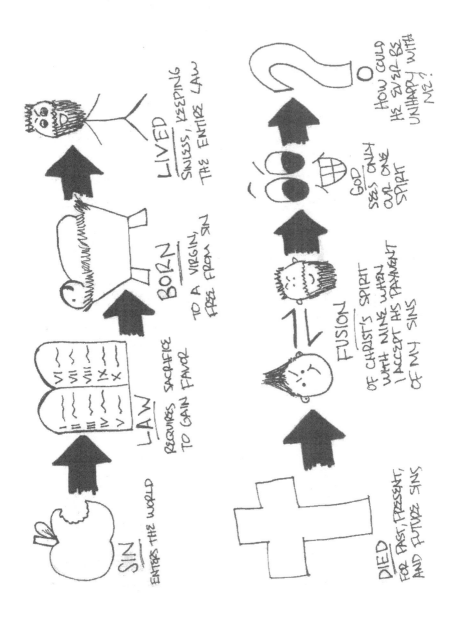

SIN
ENTERS THE WORLD

LAW
REQUIRES SACRIFICE
TO GAIN FAVOR

BORN
TO A VIRGIN,
FREE FROM SIN

LIVED
SINLESS, KEEPING
THE ENTIRE LAW

DIED
FOR PAST, PRESENT,
AND FUTURE SINS

FUSION
OF CHRIST'S SPIRIT
WITH MINE WHEN
I ACCEPT HIS PAYMENT
OF MY SINS

GOD
SEES ONLY
OUR ONE
SPIRIT

HOW COULD
HE EVER BE
UNHAPPY WITH
ME?

Sin came into the world and separated us from God. Then came the law that required sacrifices to be right with God. That was much better than the alternative of never knowing if He was pleased with you. Then came little baby Jesus, born to a virgin, under the law. He grew up to be manly bearded Jesus and lived a perfect life, keeping and teaching the law. He died as a perfect sacrifice for ALL sin; past, present, and future. At the time all of my sins were future sins seeing as how I wasn't born yet so I'm really glad He tagged on that last one. When I accept Christ's sacrifice as my own, He and I become one[11] (see me with the little Mohawk and gauges?). His spirit fuses with my spirit and "Jessus" (Jesus + Jess) is born. That means when God looks at me, He doesn't just see me, or see Jesus mostly and a little bit of me. No, we are one, so when He looks at me he sees our oneness. All HIS righteousness, all HIS holiness, and all of HIS perfection, one with me! How then, can He be anything but completely pleased with me at all times?

I know while you are reading this you may be thinking, "Well, you had me until those last couple of pictures. I'm not sure if I believe those!" I understand that completely, I was right there with you the first time I heard this too. Stick with me, I plan on having my fellow doubters won over by the time you get to the end of this book. The first thing we need to do is discover our

---

[11] 1 Corinthians 6:17

freedom from having to do things, even good things, to receive from God.

9
Laying Down the Law

Believe it or not the Law is what laid the foundation for grace. At the time it was given it offered hope because it allowed you to have peace with God through sacrifice. Though it only lasted until the next time you sinned, it was the better than the alternative, never knowing if you had good standing with Him. So, what is "The Law" exactly?

The Law is the ultimate list and do's and don'ts. It's God's standard of perfection. The Law is all inclusive, you can't choose to keep some of it and not other parts; it's all or nothing. The Law measures and sets expectations. It is really good at revealing failures and short comings. The Law is only satisfied by sacrifice. It is black and white, straight forward, and without loop holes. The Law is the arch enemy of the imperfect.

If you want to find the Law just flip over to Exodus 19-24 and you will find the giving of the Law. Also, the entire book of Leviticus and quite a bit of Deuteronomy is dedicated to the Law. There are 208 blessings and 365 curses in the Law. There is literally more punishment than reward that comes with living under the Law.

The Law contains some great guidelines for living; for instance, the Ten Commandments. It's good to know that we probably shouldn't murder people or that we should honor our father and mother. The Law also contains some extreme forms of punishment when you don't live within those guidelines. One particularly disturbing punishment for me personally is what the Law says should be done to rebellious and stubborn children.

> **"If a person has a stubborn, rebellious son who pays no attention to his father or mother, and they discipline him to no avail, his father and mother must seize him and bring him to the elders at the gate of his city. They must declare to the elders of his city, 'Our son is stubborn and rebellious and pays no attention to what we say—he is a glutton and drunkard.' Then all the men of his city must stone him to death. In this way you will purge out wickedness from among you, and all Israel will hear about it and be afraid. "[12]**

Passages like that one remind me how exceedingly thankful I am that my parents didn't decided to live by the Law because I would have been stoned extremely early

---

[12] Deuteronomy 21:18-21 (NET)

on! The problem with the Law is that if you choose to live under it you have to live under all of it. You must believe in and adhere to the Ten Commandments as well as the stoning of your little rebels. Every failure, even the smallest ones, had a penalty of death. Death is what we deserve when we live in imperfection; the Law's only power is to reveal that. Life could be regained through sacrifice, but even those had rules and specifics you had to follow in order for it to be good enough for God to accept it.

"'Now if his offering is a peace offering sacrifice, if he presents an offering from the herd, he must present before the Lord a flawless male or a female. He must lay his hand on the head of his offering and slaughter it at the entrance of the Meeting Tent, and the sons of Aaron, the priests, must splash the blood against the altar's sides. Then the one presenting the offering must present a gift to the Lord from the peace offering sacrifice: He must remove the fat that covers the entrails and all the fat that surrounds the entrails, the two kidneys with the fat on their sinews, and the protruding lobe on the liver (which he is to remove along with the kidneys). Then the sons of Aaron must offer it up in smoke on the altar atop the burnt offering that is on the wood in the fire as a gift of a soothing aroma to the Lord."[13]

---

[13] Leviticus 3:1-5 (NET)

Those are some strict, extremely precise standards that are set for redemption. I have a feeling I'd be out of luck if I had to remember all the rules for every different kind of sacrifice I had to offer for every single sin I committed. We look at this, gasp at how extreme it is, and sigh in relief that we don't live under it anymore. Why is it that we are free from living that way? Why is it even in the Bible if we don't have to follow that anymore?

The latter question burned in my mind for quite some time as there grew in me a growing desire to rip the entire Old Testament out of my Bible and throw it away. Then, I discovered something beautiful. Without the law, we would be unable to see the fullness and glory of grace. Without our inability to be enough on our own there would be no need for Jesus. How could we understand the depth of God's love for us without first understanding the depth of our brokenness?

Jesus's purpose was not to have an Old Testament burning party. He did not come to do away with or abolish the law. He came to complete it. Jesus, himself, even said, **"Do not think that I have come to abolish the Law or the Prophets; I have not come to abolish them but to fulfill them."**[14] He was the final perfect, complete, sufficient, and ultimately pleasing sacrifice that completed the law and gave us the gift of righteousness so that we

---

[14] Matthew 5:17

could be free from the law. Life, redemption, freedom, they came to us the only way they could—through a perfect sacrifice innocently and willingly made.

When Adam sinned in the garden, death came as a result of his failure. Right away this is seen as God must shed blood to make clothes for covering Adam and Eve's nakedness.[15] When Jesus comes, He brings life in the midst of our failure, despite our actions.[16] The moment of his death is even marked with bodies rising from their graves, filled with new found life.[17]

Everything comes full circle as Jesus becomes the final sacrifice that will ever have to be made. All the rebels like me let out a big, "Hell, yeah!" as we run towards our freedom from that system. The faithful church goers let out a controlled but hearty "Amen." Even so, with our excited shouts and nods of agreement, you can walk into churches all across America and hear the message of law being preached from pulpits. It seems that we have now traded the entirety of the Law for a balance of Law plus grace. Let's do the math on that shall we?

Law + Grace = Law

Little bit of law + Massive amounts of grace = Law

---

[15] Genesis 3:21
[16] Romans 5:13-17
[17] Matthew 27:52

One sentence of law + an encyclopedia set of grace = Law

Mixing Law and grace is like coming in after a hard day of working out in the yard, drenched in sweat and parched from the heat. Your spouse meets you at the door with a nice, big, refreshing glass of ice water. Right as you are about to gulp down your much needed refreshment they say, "Oh, by the way, I dropped a little bit of poison in there on accident. It's mostly water though so it should be fine!" Would you still drink that water? Even if you knew it was just one drop of poison? Of course not! That is what we do though, we drop one little bit of Law in our grace bucket and say, "Well, it's mostly grace so it should be fine!"

You cannot mix them. You cannot live by both. If you try to mix them you will get Law and you will fail at it. I know you may be reading this thinking, "I don't know of any churches that teach that!" They are hard to spot because what they teach lines up with how the world works and how our minds function, but so many of the churches today that claim Christ's name are teaching what I like to call "Law Remix." It is equally as damaging and brings just as much perceived separation from God as the old Law did, while taking on the façade of something different; a wolf in grace clothing.

Growing up I was taught, believed, and even told people that though we no longer live under the Old Testament Law, any commands that are restated in the New Testament we must follow. If we fail to do so, God won't be mad at us, He will just be really disappointed. This makes so much sense to us as humans.

As children we become disappointed with our parents when they aren't the support we need, as friends we become disappointed when our friends let us down, as parents we feel disappointment in our children when they are disobedient, and even in our churches we become disappointed with other members, our leaders, and even our pastor when our beliefs don't match their beliefs or they fail to call and check up on us when we miss a couple of weeks. Humans are masters of disappointment.

I've heard quite a few times the metaphor of a father and a son used to illustrate this point. The father will never stop loving his son. His son may even forsake his father, run off in rebellion in the other direction, and even seek out to hurt his father. Still the father's love never changes. However, while the son's rebellion rages, the father becomes disappointed in him. He is no longer proud to say "That's my boy!" The father is filled with sadness and disappointment in who his son has become. Some say, so it is with God and us. Though He never stops loving us, He does become disappointed in who we become in our rebellion.

Out of this belief is born a religion driven by the desire to never end up as a disappointment. It manifests itself in churches in the form of lists. Lists of what to do, how to act, what kind of a person to be, what to believe, how to dress, what unbelievers look like, and how to make God happy when you fail to keep your lists. It produces Christians addicted to their religion and motivated by duty, living in fear until their next fix. What you get are religion junkies visiting their dealer every Sunday morning.

I may be speaking from my own experiences when I call this dedication to religion addiction. I find it interesting, however, that when you look at the definition of "addiction" such a life fits within it.

Addiction = the state of being enslaved to a habit or practice or to something that is psychologically or physically habit-forming, as narcotics, to such an extent that its cessation causes severe trauma.[18]

---

[18] Webster's Dictionary

I have been a religion addict. I was **enslaved** to a **habit** to an extent that I was afraid if I stopped living up to these rules and expectations I wouldn't be good enough for God. It amazes me how many of us religion addicts are out there. There really should be a Religion Addicts Anonymous; I'd be the first to sign up!

So many lecture about how other addictions are evil and people who live such lifestyles are outside of God's blessing. I have to argue that any addiction is destructive whether it be an addiction to rules or to booze. Jesus' message was all about freedom not slavery. He came to give us a religion detox and free us from its enslavement. We are free from the power of sin and the punishment of it. We are free from having to earn God's favor. We are free from sin and we are free to sin.

It is in our own minds that we are a disappointment to him. It makes sense to us that our evil deeds separate us from him. In reality, it's quite the opposite, we feel separate from him so we do evil things.[19] Jesus died to free us from the law remix just as much as he died to free us from the original law.

In order to help retrain our minds and unlearn our law remix we need to identify some things we've heard in

---

[19] Colossians 1:21-22

church that aren't really true. I've spent almost my entire life in church and I've heard some pretty interesting things spoken from pulpits, pews, and the people who fill them. There are some common myths that float around church, old wives tales about who God is and how he relates to us. The following are a few myths that are familiar to me from my time spent in church and how taking in the radical extravagance of grace busted each one of them.

My relationship with God is perfect but my fellowship with him gets messed up when I sin.

This, my friends, is what I fondly call the "Christian Nitpick." We carefully pick our words to justify teaching that we need to do good things to get God's blessing without actually admitting that's what we're doing. Though it does make sense in the human mind that our failures cause God sadness or disappointment, God doesn't work the same way that we do. God has never done things the way we do them so what makes us think He's going to start with this one? It's so easy for us to think that because we feel distant from God that means He is upset with us. In reality that is us pulling away from Him; never is it Him forsaking us. We are 100% right with God, fellowship, relationship, and any other ships.[20]

God turned His back on Jesus while he was on the cross.

---

[20] Colossians 1:22-23

Can anyone tell me where in the Bible it actually says this? No, you can't, because it's not in there. What happens is we read Jesus' exclamation of, "My God, my God, why have you forsaken me?" and we interpret it using our humanity. I think we interpret it this was because we have this idea that God can't be in the presence of sin. Which really doesn't make sense if you think about it because, I mean, God and Satan had a face to face throw down over Job and I'm pretty sure no one could argue that Satan is sinless.

My thoughts on this particular myth are that Jesus' statement of "My God, my God why have you forsaken me?"[21] was exactly how Jesus felt at that moment. The weight of the world's sin was on his shoulders as well as all the guilt, shame, and disgust that comes with sin. How many times have you felt as if God has forsaken you? The reality is, He is still right there, holding you in His arms, you just can't feel it in that moment.

God expects us to give 10% of our earnings as offering.

First off, giving out of duty is without meaning and if you are doing it expecting God to bless you for your pennies in the plate then you have completely missed the point of Jesus. Secondly, Paul makes it pretty clear in 2 Corinthians that it's not about the amount you give but

---

[21] Matthew 27:46

simply that it's out of the desire of your heart. God loves a cheerful giver.[22]

Extremes are bad.

This is the epitome of mixing Law and grace together before we serving it to the world in the name of balance. We chant "everything in moderation, nothing in excess" as if that phrase came straight from the mouth of Jesus. Pastors who preach the harshness of God frown on the ones who are too mushy and filled with emotion and vice versa. God lives in the extremes. He is all inclusive in his grace, excessive in his love, and irresponsible in his forgiveness.

God is disappointed, sad, or mad at me if I'm not doing the things a Christian should do.

Whatever way you spin it, the belief/teaching that God is in any way affected by us, that His mood is dependent on our behavior, is completely unbiblical and makes Him out to be emotionally fragile and distant. God is not and never will be anything but completely pleased with you. Jesus's payment was for ALL sins. Not just the ones we're sorry for, not just the ones we do good things to make up for, but ALL sins. Nothing can separate us from his love.[23]

---

[22] 2 Corinthians 9:7
[23] Romans 8:38-39

Jesus disliked the Pharisees because they taught and followed the law.

I think it's important to be aware that even us radical gracers can teach and believe some myths about Christ. As I mentioned earlier, once won over by the extremity of grace one might be tempted to see the Law as evil. Jesus taught and followed the law. Wait... what?! Yep, He did! So... does that mean Jesus disliked himself? No, he taught and lived the Law in its purist form.

Jesus's issue with the Pharisees wasn't their teaching of the Law. His issue with them was with their inserting of human tradition and regulation into the law so that it was easier to follow. The point of the law was your inability to keep it and your need for sacrifice to make you right with God. This is why Jesus makes statements like, "You have heard that it was said, 'You shall not commit adultery.' But I tell you that anyone who looks at a woman lustfully has already committed adultery with her in his heart"[24] In this moment he is essentially saying to them, "Oh you think the standard is keeping this rule, let me tell you what the actual standard is." Jesus always has and always will be about people's hearts; this is the reason he was willing to die for our freedom, he knew we'd never be able to gain it on our own and we were never meant to!

---

[24] Matthew 5:27-28

Have you heard any of these myths in church? Have they shaped your belief of who God is and how He sees you? Do you have trouble believing that these aren't true? I understand. I've been there.

There is one thing of which I am resolutely sure and that is that I have never been more confident in anything than I am in the fact that God sees me as perfect, offers me freedom, and demands nothing from me. I will gladly sacrifice all I am and all I have for that truth, not because it's expected of me but because of the depth of desire it creates within me.

How then, do we recover from our religion addiction? How should we live now? If I'm free to sin does that mean I should do whatever I want and not worry about being good or bad? Won't people sin more if we teach them they are free?

Our next step is to check into religion rehab starting with our very first Religion Addicts Anonymous meeting.

11

Paper Millionaires

As most know, and as is often said jokingly, the first step in recovery is admitting you have a problem. The second step closely follows, and that is coming to the realization that there is a power greater than ourselves that can restore us to sanity. You must first become broken and then come to the realization that it will take something outside of and greater than yourself to put you back together.

For me, and I would say many addicts, those are two pretty big steps. They require facing the reality of your brokenness as well as taking a huge dose of humility to make those first steps. That seems to be the biggest obstacle for those coming out of religious addiction as well.

For a long time I didn't understand why people didn't want freedom. I couldn't comprehend why someone would choose to live a life based on their own accomplishments. Why would you want to live in that system? I didn't understand this at all until I began carpooling with my mom to work.

My mom is truly an amazing woman. I treasure her more now than I ever did when I was in high school, when our conflicting personality types caused us to grow apart. She graduated from high school when she was only seventeen, worked several jobs during college to pay her way through, married my dad, and continued to work to build something great for our family. She was the classic over achiever in high school and college. This translated to a pursuer of excellence in the work place as she grew older and a desire to keep the lists presented to her by the church.

As Dad and I cannonballed into grace, she waded carefully into its waters. I would get so frustrated with her because she held so tightly to achievements within the faith. I tried to be patient, though, as she has so often been with me. She's catching up to us on her grace journey and we talk more about it now.

It wasn't until one early morning commute that I began to understand what made it so difficult for her. She mentioned to me that if she believed in grace like we did that would mean all the things she worked so hard for meant nothing anymore. All her hours of service, dedication to Bible study, and hours spent giving into youth ministry gave her no more favor from God than the tattooed, biker dude who just accepted Christ and still spends his nights partying.

For those of us who, when faced with the reality of being inadequate, run as far from God as we can, grace is a welcome relief from the emptiness. There are others though who have power, meaning, and worth built up in the system of earning God's favor and for them it's much more difficult to forsake that system for one that levels the playing field. In fact, living by that system allows us to stay in control, pull our own strings, and control our own reward... or so we think.

Imagine if you had spent your entire life working and saving and storing away your money because your dream was to become a millionaire. Then, finally, after all your hard work you reach your first million and are filled with pride and joy at what you have accomplished.

Then, much to your dismay, an evil government takes over and announces that all money is obsolete and they will only accept payment for things in the form of chocolate bars. You think to yourself, "No! I'm a millionaire! I've worked hard for what I have!" You might even try to buy things with your stored up millions, but you are continually met with the disappointment of its worthlessness.

In much the same way, those who find power within a system driven by doing see no need for grace.

They cling to their millions of good deeds, accomplished quiet times, souls won for the cause, tracts passed out, and hours volunteered to services thinking that is somehow what gains God's favor.

How silly we are to think our "great" acts of service could even compare to Christ's sacrifice for us! Yet, every time we wade deeper into the waters of duty driven religion we push his sacrifice aside as if what we have to offer is better. Then we go before God and we say, "Look, I'm a millionaire! Look what I've earned!"

All he sees are paper piles set before him and he responds with, "No, but look, here I've given you the biggest chocolate bar ever, all you have to do is take it and you will have all you will ever need!" Still, we refuse, trying desperately to cling to what we think is worth more.

It's a struggle that has been going on in the church since the beginning. That's why we find Paul telling the Galatians not to set aside grace because if we could earn righteousness on our own then Christ died for nothing.[25] Then later on he tells them to stop forsaking the freedom found in Christ and returning to bondage![26]

---

[25] Galatians 2:21
[26] Galatians 5:1

We cannot earn, do, achieve, or be anything greater than what Christ has already done and made us. We have to open our eyes to the worthlessness of our paper millions and see the riches of grace that have already been given to us.

It's fairly easy to tell when you are living a life of law remix and stockpiling paper millions because it shows up in your relationships. You believe that God relates to you based on your performance so you relate to others based on theirs. Some telltale signs of living in law are the following:

- You are constantly comparing yourself to others
- You are afraid to be honest with those around you because they may think less of you
- You expect things back from others when you do good things for them- this can even be as innocent as expecting a thank you for a gift or kindness when you forgive a hurt
- You feel wronged if others don't work as hard as you do
- You are driven by and control others around you with guilt
- You feel the need to constantly point out to others how they need to improve
- You are easy to anger and slow to forgive

These will quickly creep into your relationships because you will always relate based on how you perceive that you are related to. God doesn't relate to us that way. We are called out of a life driven by performance into the unwarranted, all-encompassing, never ending grace of Christ. It's time that we find freedom by embracing that we have been made new!

12 Rebels and Revolutionaries

I have always been intrigued by the image of the Phoenix. This mythological creature that is born from its death moved something within me. I find it relatable. Most times in my life before I have been able to progress, something first must die within me. On my journey to sobriety, my love for alcohol had to die. Upon discovering grace, my desire for justice had to die. In my pursuit of honesty, my fear had to die. There has been much death in my life along my journey; followed each time by the birth of something greater and more beautiful than the deceased.

We sing songs about beautiful things being made from dust and beautiful things rising from ashes but we are afraid to become dust. From the very beginning of man God was in the business of taking something crushed, dirty, and unimportant and breathing life into it.

In the story of the Phoenix, the sun looks down and sees a beautiful bird and calls it out to be his special bird. The bird worships the sun and vows its undying loyalty to him. Times goes on and the Phoenix becomes old and worn, tattered by time. It cries out to the sun to make it new again but there is no answer. So the Phoenix flies back to its homeland where it first met the sun and it makes a nest and rests. Then it cries out again to the sun for renewal. This time the sun hears it and begins to beat down on it with all the heat it can muster. The other animals run and hide from the harsh rays of the sun. Through the pain of the heat, the Phoenix stays until finally it burst into flames. The fire subsides and all that can be seen is a pile of ash. Slowly, the ashes begin to move and a new, even more beautiful young Phoenix rises from them.[27]

Life brings fire, pain, heartache, and we fight being broken. We fight being reduced to ash, being crushed to dust, not because we can stop it but because we are afraid to let everyone see us as imperfect. We are even afraid to let God see us as imperfect. Silly us. He looks down at our ashes and sees a brand new beautiful child rising from them. Where we see dust He breathes in life making something lovely. We pretend that we are whole because we don't see our brokenness as being enough for Him. We forget so easily that we were born from brokenness; brokenness that He came in and made perfect.

The more we embrace the fire, the more we are willing to become dust, the more we will see something beautiful being made from it. Rebirth looks different for

---

[27] Mythology: Timeless Tales of God's and Heroes, Edith Hamilton

different people, but for me it came in the death of the rebel and the birth of the revolutionary.

I was always so aggressive; always looking for a fight and usually finding one. There was an excessive amount of anger and resentment towards people in my life, especially authority figures. I hated being tied down to silly rules that I saw as just another way to brain wash and control me. I was surrounded by structure and that made me crave chaos. I found myself constantly bucking the rider and throwing the reins. I became known as, as well as self-proclaimed, a rebel. For a long time I felt completely justified in my rebellion because I was hurting.

Through my journey of maturity and healing, I learned, mainly by failing, many life lessons; one of the biggest being that rebels don't change the world. All rebels do is create chaos fueled by bitter, angry people that know how to tear down the walls of injustice but have no idea how to build something from the rubble. Rebels fight wars but don't know what to do after they win them. They fight simply for the sake of fighting. I began to realize that being a rebel didn't accomplish what I wanted it to.

I remained fiery and continued to push the lines but I learned how to do it in a way that pushed people towards change instead of just created chaos. My first summer after graduating from college I went to youth camp as an adult leader. The week's theme was about being a revolutionary. That's when it clicked for me.

See, there's a difference between a rebel and a revolutionary. A rebel just resists authority for the sake of the resisting; a revolutionary resists in order to make a change. I have always claimed a rebel heart but I am being transformed into a revolutionary. There is much that needs changing in our world, in our churches, in our Christian schools... and I want to start a revolution. I want a revolution that frees people from the oppression of religious nonsense that Christ never supported. I want a revolution that pushes our churches to pursue love and grace over guilt and greed. I want a revolution that causes Christian schools to produce kids that desire a depth with God instead of those that just go through the motions so as not to be caught out of line. It's time for a change in our world. It's time for us to stand up and start a revolution.

The revolution starts within your own heart. It begins with retraining your mind to process things with a grace filter. Remember, you must take in grace before you can give it out to others. Don't be afraid to let a revolutionary rise from the ashes.

13

Partying with Sinners

      I have an iPhone and it is pretty much glued to my side at all times. It is my camera, my phone, at times my computer, and even my flash light. It does almost everything and for the things it doesn't, you can install apps.

      There are apps for everything from games to money management to photo editing. It's amazing to have access to everything you need right there in the palm of your hand. Some apps are tricky though. For instance, I wanted to play a certain game so I searched for it in the App Store and, lucky me, it's a free game! I started playing it and, of course, the addict in me kicked in and I spent hours upon hours determined to beat the game.

      Finally, banners wave, confetti flies, and I do my victory dance. As the confetti clears, I read the words, "To complete the game buy the full version for only $1.99!" What?! NO! I thought this was a free game?! That's not fair! What a clever trick it is, enticing me with its claim that it costs me nothing and then after I'm caught up in the game... BOOM! Pay up!

We do that within the church as well. Before you're a Christian you are lured in with promises of acceptance and reassurances that Jesus loves everyone. Then the moment you get caught up in the game it's time to pay up. It's almost as if as soon as you come up from the water you are met with a list of do's and don'ts, rules to becoming a better Christian. People like me are confused. We question, "But... I thought Jesus loved everyone even in my sin?" We are met with answers like "Well, yes but God isn't happy with you if you're sinning! Yes, but, it makes God sad when we sin! Yes, but, your fellowship with God will suffer! Yes, but..."

So how does God deal with sin?

First, it's important to know what sin is. That may sound silly because everyone knows what sin is. Even people who don't believe in the existence of God have some sort of moral compass that lets them know when something is right or wrong. Paul takes it a little further when defining sin for us.

In Romans, he says anything that is not from faith is sin.[28] That means anything we do, even good things, out of fear or obligation is sin. If we go to church on Sunday

---

[28] Romans 14:23

because we have to or because we're afraid God will be sad if we don't, then we are sinning. Sin is not just the blatantly obvious disobedience of moral code such as murder, deception, or adultery. Sin is also what we propagate in churches under the guise of service. Sin doesn't just lurk in the back corners of dark alleys; it sometimes sits with its hands raised in our church services.

Romans says we have been declared righteous and we have peace with God because of Christ's sacrifice.[29] Paul also mentions in Romans that even though we are all sinners, we are justified (made right) freely and by the grace that comes through faith in Christ.[30] Later on Paul writes that God is no longer counting our sins against us.[31] Hebrews clears up all question about which sins exactly are covered under Christ's sacrifice by the statement, **"...But now he has appeared once for all at the consummation of the ages to put away sin by his sacrifice."**[32]

Jesus died over 2000 years ago so unless we believe that none of our sins were covered we have to believe that His death covered past, present, and future sins. Still we seem to think that His death only covers all the sins we commit until we become Christians and then

---

[29] Romans 5:1
[30] Romans 3:23-24
[31] Romans 4:7-8
[32] Hebrews 9:26

we have to beg forgiveness every time we mess up for fear of punishment.

The most common response to that is a question. "So, then, you believe we are free to just do whatever we want and God isn't going to be mad at us?!"

Yes. I do believe that.

We are 100% perfect. We are 100% righteous before God. He doesn't even remember our sin![33] We are absolutely free to do anything we want without punishment from God.

Why would we want to do that though? The purpose of grace is freedom! All sin does is enslave you. Why would you want to use freedom to gain slavery?[34] Such a question was asked by the early Christians in the church at Corinth. Paul wrote them saying that though all is lawful, not all is beneficial for them.[35] I am free, because of Christ, to get drunk every night if that is my desire, but why would I want to be so bound to something that brings me nothing but pain and captivity? Live free, but don't let your freedom lead you down roads that will only bring you

---

[33] Hebrews 10:17
[34] Galatians 5:1
[35] I Corinthians 6:12

pain.[36] When He says something is free there is no extra $1.99 payment at the end of the game. If you feel yourself weighed down by the false freedom found within the church walls, don't worry. God has an app for that. It's called grace.

So then, knowing that there is now no longer any condemnation for our sin, how do we deal with "sinners" or those outside the church? For the answer to this question I look to the ultimate example. I look at how Jesus treated sinners.

Jesus is the king of hanging with the wrong crowd. When he walked this earth, He was constantly getting griped at by the religious leaders for partying with the wrong people, calling the riff-raff his friends, and crossing the social boundaries. His response was, "Hey, these are the people who need me!"[37]

Jesus is found being a refuge for an accused prostitute facing death[38] and eating dinner with tax collectors.[39] He even allows a prostitute to anoint his feet with oil, forgives her sins, and then later has dinner at her house with her sister. Then after that he raises her

---

[36] I Peter 2:16
[37] Luke 5:31
[38] John 8:1-11
[39] Luke 19:1-10

brother from the dead![40] Now that is some excessive love for someone caught so tightly in sin.

How then do we follow his example?

As one who has been one of those sinners, I know what changes people. I know what changed me. It wasn't a pointing out of my sins, a display of how I needed to change, or the phrase "I'm praying for you." I was painfully aware of my sins, and I didn't need to be reminded of them. I was very in tune with the fact that I was broken. I knew I was dirty. I knew I was hard to deal with. What changed me was not the statement of those facts. What changed me were the people in my life who purposed to pour love into me at my most unworthy moments. What changed me was people who showed me who I really was, who God said I was.

See, because really, I wasn't broken. I wasn't dirty. I wasn't a lost cause.

I was made right. I was whole. I was loved. I was beautiful. I was pure. I was treasured. I was perfect. I just couldn't see that. I acted out of who I thought I was.

---

[40] Luke 7:37, Luke 10:38-42, John 11:2

Our job within the church is not to tell people they are sinners. Trust me, they already know that. Our job is to help them see who they really are. Our job is to show them how much they are loved, how perfect God sees them, and how much peace there is in that knowledge. Our job is to bring them life not to remind them of their death.

I have one of the most amazing best friends on the planet. I am constantly amazed by how persistent her love is for me. I am, admittedly, a little rougher around the edges. I curse too much and have a fiery heart, but she loves me. She has never tried to change me or water me down or even tell me what I need to be better at. She just accepts me and is proud of me and believes in me, and it makes me want to be a better person.

I hang out with her, share life with her, and watch how she treats other people with grace every day. I experience how she lavishes love onto me even in my failures. It's in these moments that I am inspired to be good, get better, and show others love.

How then do we deal with sinners?

Simply love them. Love them with all that you have in you. Show them every day who they are. Remind them in every moment what they are worth. Let their sin be the last thing you worry about, and instead focus on showing them they are free from it. Give grace, lavish love, and don't let fear keep you from being a light of love to those in desperate need of the hope you have to offer.

Destemido

Fear is Satan's favorite weapon. He loves for fear to jump in the driver's seat of our lives because it steals our peace, prohibits honesty, and makes us believe that God is upset with us. Fear is a powerful and driving force in our world and in our churches.

Everyone has fears, it's the natural make up of a human being. No one had to tell you to be afraid. You just were. From the moment you heard that clap of thunder that sent you running to the safety of your parent's bed, you knew how to fear. As we grow up our fears begin to change. The fear of the storm becomes a fear of being a good enough mom so your children will run to you during it. Fear takes on a different face and it reaches into every part of our lives, especially our relationships. It all starts with how we think God relates to us because how we think God relates to us is how we will relate to others.

I was never a big fan of the repetition of the phrase "fear God" that I heard in the church. I most certainly was afraid of him, afraid I wasn't good enough, afraid he was always angry with me, or afraid he was constantly waiting to punish me every time I screwed up. Any time I would dare to express those feelings I would be met with the answer, "Well, that's not what fearing God means." Church people like to define that phrase as "respect for God."

They always used that analogy about a child who touches a hot stove and gets burned, then he learns to respect the stove's power so he doesn't touch it anymore. My immediate thought was always, "No, he got hurt that's why he's not touching it, duh!" No, I think fearing God is much more than that. I don't think God operates by burning his followers when they reach out to touch him. In fact, in Romans, it says that when we receive His spirit we are freed from the spirit of slavery that leads to fear.[41]

With things like this, I think we miss out because we speak English. When I say. "I fear spiders" and when I say, "I fear God" they sound the same. Similarly, I say I love my dad and I love coffee, but do you really think I love coffee as much as I love my dad? Of course not! They have very different meanings and different depth even though they are the same word. Doesn't English just really mess things up sometimes?

---

[41] Romans 8:15

There are two different meanings of the word "fear" in the dictionary. The first one is what we always think of when we hear the word fear, "a distressing emotion aroused by impending danger, evil, pain, etc., whether the threat is real or imagined; the feeling or condition of being afraid."[42] Common sense, right? There's a second definition of fear though, one that has a different meaning entirely, and it is this: "reverential awe."[43]

The first form of fear is a deadly one. It will destroy relationships, dreams, and self-esteem. If you live in fear of God, that he will withhold blessings if you fail and strike you down when you don't measure up, then you will only end up depressed, worn out, and frustrated. If you live a life driven by fear it will keep you from chasing your dreams, being real with those around you, and even giving love to the people closest to you. It can destroy marriages, wound your children, and make you feel worthless. That kind of fear does not come from God.

The latter definition of fear, however, is one to get excited about! Reverence in awe, those words have a little more depth than just respect. I live in zealous reverence and complete awe of God. Not because He demands it of me, but because he came to me in my brokenness and made me whole. He met me in my moments of not enough and made me perfect. He saw me when I was

---

[42] Webster's Dictionary
[43] Webster's Dictionary

most unlovable and poured his favor on me. I fear him because, though he deserves so much more, he calls the rags I offer him enough.

Which one drives you? Reverent awe that comes from desire or paralyzing fear that keeps you from living in peace? I still have moments where fear tries to take over in my life. That's why I have "Fearless" in Portuguese, "Destemido," tattooed across my wrist. We all need reminders of the power in living without fear. I urge you, my friends, to find bravery by taking in how perfect God sees you. Live fearlessly. Love extravagantly. There is freedom on the other side of fear.

15

Authenticity

One thing that living in fear makes it difficult to do is to be authentic. When our lives are driven by fear it is impossible for us to be authentic. Instead, we spend all of our time worried what others will think of us, what people might say, what kind of judgment might be shot our way if people knew who we *really* are. It's a struggle we wake up to every morning and have to face because in a world so driven by fear, so focused on getting things right, where is there room for authenticity?

I used to be really good at lying. I mean, I was REALLY good at it, to the point where I became a different person depending on who I was with at the time. I could easily dodge specific questions so that no one really knew anything deep about me. I was a master of manipulating situations to facilitate my needs. I was a chameleon, ever changing with my surroundings in an attempt to survive the jungle that is life.

On my recovery journey I was challenged to embrace a radical honesty, of sorts. It required that I give up my conman ways, which proved much more difficult than I thought it would be! I learned very quickly that the world loves liars and even more so, the church loves them.

We do, you know, we love being lied to. Of course, if we really examined this, we would never admit to the truth of it; but it is true. We walk into our well maintained buildings, with a smile on our face and a pleasant answer to every question of, "How are you?" All the while our families are falling apart and our boss is beating us down. We are burnt out, exhausted, and addicted seeing no hope of recovery. So we lie. Every Sunday, we put our mask on and grasp at holiness, shattered silhouettes dreaming of completion. And we are praised for how well we fool one another. We love the liars.

Why, you might wonder, do we love deception so much? Why do we despise authenticity? I think there are three basic reasons for this.

First, because authenticity creates vulnerability and dishonesty allows you to avoid hurt. There is never a possibility for pain if you never take off your armor. If you spend your life hiding behind a plastic version of yourself then the real you never gets any wear and tear. We fear the breaking of our hearts, so we lie.

We lie to ourselves and say we don't really care. We lie to others and tell them that we're okay. We lie to God and tell Him we believe that He loves us. We lie because the truth is just too painful. The rest of the world is content with our lies because no one wants to be vulnerable. No one wants to face that hurt. We just push it into the darkest corner of our hearts and push a plastic plant in front of it, hoping no one will see how broken we really are.

Secondly, authentic people always expose the dishonest. This fact has become quite real to me over the past few years. In a world of masks, the person who dares to take hers off will become an immediate threat to those who have grown so attached to their own. It becomes very easy to spot a counterfeit when it's right next to something genuine. When someone stands up and shares their hurts and their struggles it becomes dangerous for those who so tightly clutch their fabricated righteousness, and their false perfection is exposed for the impossibility that it is. This is why our conversations in the church scratch the surface of our behavior while our lives fall apart behind the scenes.

Finally, authenticity is hard to control. I loved being a conman because it gave me control. It allowed me to think I had some kind of say in how my life would be. I believed for so long that God was angry with me, that he demanded impossible things from me without ever giving me the ability to even begin to accomplish those things. I decided if I couldn't control how God saw me I could definitely control how other people saw me. In a way, I was right. Lying, manipulation, psychoanalyzing people, it all gave me some sort of control over how others saw me.

None of those things changed the fact that I was still a broken soul in bondage to my own beliefs. No one could help me because I made everyone believe I was fine. We do that a lot, especially in church, pretend we are fine. Honesty is harder to reign in. It doesn't sit quietly in a pew and take notes. It jumps up and says, "Hell, yeah!" at a great truth and dances to a powerful worship song.

Honesty isn't afraid to disagree with the pastor. Honesty is real, radical, raw, and in your face. Honesty doesn't stay within the boundaries. That's what makes honesty so hard to embrace. Really, we all fear being out of control.

It's interesting, to me, how authenticity always accompanies Christ. I mean, have you read some of Jesus's interactions with people? He was pretty direct! What about Paul? He definitely was not one to pull punches or sugar coat truth! More than that even, Christ attracted the broken, the hurt, the incomplete and didn't ask them to be anything but what they were. He didn't demand that they fix themselves, that they somehow get their act together first; that's what He was there for.

Should our churches not be a place that breeds authenticity? Should they not create spaces where it's ok to be honest about struggles? Shouldn't our goal be to help the hurting find healing?

It all begins with honesty. We must dare to be genuine, venture to authenticity, and risk taking off our masks. Be confident in who Christ has made you. Open your eyes to the truth of God's pleasure in you and let that ignite the desire to be honest with those around you.

You may be discouraged reading this thinking, "I want to be authentic, I the desire to, but I just can't do it. It's so difficult and no matter how hard I try I just can't" I find myself making the same argument about most things that life with Christ calls me to.

It is difficult, living a life so contrary to the way the world works, so against the grain of a life that demands and measures and expects. Most times I feel as Paul describes in Romans, "For I don't understand what I am doing. For I do not do what I want—instead, I do what I hate."[44] Such is the struggle of a holy spirit occupying a tattered body so attracted to the things that destroy it.

I am encouraged by this passage in Philippians. "For the one bringing forth in you both the desire and the effort—for the sake of his good pleasure—is God."[45] The most glorious things about God. His grace doesn't just give us desire, passion, and purpose and leave us to figure how do use all those things. Instead, Paul writes, God brings forth in us both the desire *and* the effort. In essence what he's saying here is that experiencing God's full favor, His grace, not only gives us the desire to do good things but also the ability to do them, something we fall terribly short of on our own.

So, if you find yourself desperately wanting authenticity but being doubtful of your ability to achieve it, be encouraged by the knowledge that God has given you both the desire and effort—you are not in alone in your pursuit of honesty! Find confidence in that knowledge, wear it proudly, let Christ move and work in you, and let him use you to make over our churches into places where the broken, hurt, and incomplete can come to be real.

---

[44] Romans 7:15 (NET)
[45] Philippians 2:13 (NET)

16

Deception and Old Tricks

Living in authenticity is a beautifully terrifying existence and it's also something that Satan despises for us to do. In fact, Jesus calls Satan the "father of all lies."[46] This is a fitting title for him since he enjoys using things we think are good and twisting them into something he uses to control us.

He is the master of logic and reason. He is much more aware of how God feels about us than we are so he's quite good at making us believe the opposite. He uses the same tricks, the same lies, and the same convincing stories to drive us farther and farther from seeing who we really are as he did upon his first appearance to humanity.

He made his debut in the Garden of Eden as a sly snake who seemed to know everything there was to know about God and what He thought of His two most valued creations. Upon meeting Eve, the first thing he does is make God out to be a destroyer of freedom. "Did God really say you can't eat ANY of the fruit in the garden?"[47]

---

[46] John 8:44

Interestingly enough, God said pretty much the exact opposite, "You are **free** to eat from **any** tree in the garden; but you must not eat from the tree of the knowledge of good and evil, for when you eat from it you will certainly die."[48]

After planting the seed of doubt at God's expectations of her, he tempts Eve with something she already has, god-likeness.[49] She was already created in His own image. He walked with her every day, filling her with who He was.

Satan hasn't updated his resume much. He's still telling us the same story now as he told Eve then, manipulating the truth to make us doubt just enough to think God's hiding something from us. He cunningly warps what we believe about God and ourselves in an attempt to make us live contrary to who we are.

He whispers to us that we are captive and he tempts us with freedom. He tells us we are a disappointment to God and offers us a way to appease Him. Then when we choose not to believe him, he plagues

---

[47] Genesis 3:1
[48] Genesis 2:16-17
[49] Genesis 3:5

us with guilt in an attempt to convince us it's really God who we doubted.

Guilt, such a powerful weapon in his arsenal. It can drive a person to depths of depression or it can convince them to live a life obsessed with paying penance for their mistakes. It has the power to scare people into living a life of service and it has the power to drive people to a life a sin. It reaches into every part of our lives as every failure echoes with the voice naming us, "Guilty." All the while he convinces us that voice is God.

That is not God's voice.

It's interesting, if you read what happens after Adam and Eve fall for Satan's trick, how God responds. See, Adam and Eve feel guilt and shame for what they have done. They run and hide, trying desperately to cover their nakedness with crumbling shrubbery. I'm sure they feared what God would have to say to them. They had, after all, bought into a lie about who God was.

God knew. He saw them hiding, running away, afraid. Still, He comes, like every day before that one, to spend time with them, to pour out His love on them. Still he comes to be with them even in the midst of their utter failure. Even in the midst of their doubting Him.

Then He sheds blood and makes a better covering for their nakedness, for their shame. He has done the same for us. This time, He shed His own blood to cleanse the mess that we made, covering the nakedness of our sin.

God does not name us guilty; He names us righteous. Our old self, the one who was guilty, is gone and something new stands in its place. We have been made right with God and we will never be called guilty by him again.[50]

Be cautious of Satan and his shrewdness; don't let him convince you his voice is that of God's. Don't let guilt keep you from loving the unlovable and forgiving the unforgiveable. Find freedom in knowing that you are forgiven so that you can give it out to those around you.

---

[50] 2 Corinthians 5:17-21

The F Word

Forgiveness, for me at least, is probably the hardest part of living in grace. I'm really great at accepting forgiveness but not so much at giving it out to the people who have hurt me. I'm more of a "I don't like you and you don't like me so let's just never speak again" person.

For a long time I justified it by telling myself I needed to set boundaries, be wary of being hurt again, and not let myself be taken advantage of. All those things were true in the tenderness of my healing but as I grew in grace I still found myself using the same excuses.

I also became distrusting and harsh towards people who in any way resembled those who had hurt me. I withheld forgiveness thinking it gave me power over those who had hurt me while in actuality it allowed them to maintain power over me. It kept me from trusting, loving, being honest, and feeling safe.

It's funny how we think that refusing someone forgiveness gives us power. If you think about it half the people you are denying it to don't know and the other half really don't care. The only person we hurt is ourselves. We punch ourselves and expect the other person to get a black eye.

Even knowing that, we find forgiveness to be just plain hard! So we try to make it easier and we compartmentalize forgiveness deciding who we "have to" forgive and who it's okay not to forgive.

We use excuses like mine and tell ourselves that some people have just hurt us too much to be shown grace. We even expect those people to show remorse before we offer them forgiveness. Jesus seemed to have quite a different view on forgiveness.

He said crazy things about it like "love your enemies and pray for those who persecute you."[51] That's taking forgiveness to a whole other level. He doesn't say, "Forgive the people who beg for forgiveness" or "forgive those that seem really sorry" or even "forgive the ones that are no longer hurting you." No, he says love your enemies. He says pray for those who are actively trying to cause harm to you.

Jesus doesn't just tell us this; He shows us how it's done.

---

[51] Matthew 5:44

There He was, beaten within an inch of His life, condemned to death by the people who were supposed to be his religious advisors. He was abandoned by His friends and turned on by His people. The same people that flocked from miles away to hear Him speak and beg Him to heal them shouted, "Crucify Him!" He hung there naked and mangled from the aftermath of His beatings, and every breath came with excruciating pain. He looked down to see men gambling over His clothes and His response is astounding. He fought through what must have been unimaginable pain to cry out on their behalf, "Father, forgive them, for they know not what they do."[52]

The ultimate example of not just forgiveness but a lavishing of love onto those whose only desire was to cause him pain.

The first time my pastor brought those passages to my attention my immediate response was, "Well, I'm not Jesus! I can't do what He did!" An understanding smile spread across his face as he answered, "Yes, you can."

He's right. Jesus and I are one. I have His spirit moving and working in me. I have just as much power to show that kind of forgiveness as he did. I have the ability

---

[52] Luke 23:34

and opportunity to lavish love on my persecutors just like he did. To be quite honest, I'm not there yet, but I find joy in knowing the possibility is there.

Growing up, my little brother and I were very close and despite a five year age difference we always found something to imagine, pretend, and play together. The most common thing we did together was play "super heroes" which I later discovered says quite a bit about our personalities. We both have passionate hearts for the underdogs, unwanted, and weak spirited. The difference between Chance and I is how that passion in our hearts pours out.

When we were little, my super hero was Super Tommy. He was tough, strong willed, bent the rules, and (of course) had no weaknesses. Chance's super hero was Super Rascal. He was soft hearted, brave, had integrity, and had one weakness that only the people closest to him knew about. Super Tommy always scoffed at Super Rascal claiming that his tender heart made him weaker, but in the end Super Rascal somehow ended up saving Super Tommy from some kind of trouble that his hot temper had gotten him in.

As we grew up we stopped playing super heroes and we became our super heroes. I became that tough, strong willed, hot head, who strived for imperviousness.

Chance became soft hearted, brave, full of integrity, and honest about his weaknesses with the people closest to him. I often saw his tenderness as weakness, but many times he has saved me from the trouble that my hot temper has gotten me in.

We both have a strong desire to protect the weak and punish the oppressors, but where I tend to come in with aggression he comes in with love. As I am progressing on this journey of grace I find myself getting very angry with the teachers of law. I am disgusted by their words, turned off by their actions, and infuriated with their teachings. In these moments my super hero complex kicks in and I rush in to save the day; not to comfort the hurting but to punish the hurters. Chance comes in behind me taking care of the broken people that I have passed over in my rush to execute justice. I don't see Super Rascal as weak any more.

If we become so focused on punishing the oppressors that we forsake the oppressed then we miss the whole point of who Jesus was. It's interesting to me that Jesus rarely answered questions presented to him about the law with actual answers but rather responded with more questions (which I find quite annoying at times)! There is one instance where he gives a pretty straightforward answer.

A teacher of the law asks him what the greatest Commandment is and Jesus replies, "The most important commandment is this: 'Listen, O Israel! The Lord our God is the one and only Lord and you must love the Lord your God with all your heart, all your soul, all your mind, and all your strength.' The second is equally important: 'Love your neighbor as yourself.' No other commandment is greater than these."[53] What was most important to Jesus? Proving he was right and the religious leaders were wrong? Bringing those people to justice?

Love. Just love.

I understand why now. If you have love then all that other stuff falls into place. That's why it is so important because if you don't have love you can't have all that other stuff. You can't do anything right, be enough, pray enough, read your Bible enough, witness enough, tithe enough, or be "Christian" enough. If you have all those things but don't have love then what are they worth?

I continually have to refocus my mind to love the hurting instead of punish the hurters. See, because grace is for the robber and the robbed; the murderer and murdered; the raped and the rapist; the persecuted and the persecutor; the judged and the judgers; the proud and

---

[53] Mark 12:29-31

the humble; Hitler and those he killed; grace is even for those who try to suppress it. That's the beauty of grace. It makes life not fair.

The same is true of forgiveness. Forgiveness isn't just for the people who have done enough to get it. If that were the case then none of us deserve it. We have all been liars and lied to; we have all been heart breakers and heartbroken; we have all been sinners and sinned against. How can we determine who has and hasn't earned forgiveness. We need to retrain our minds to be givers of grace rather than demanders of justice. You might just find that forgiveness frees more in you than you thought was captive.

18

Peter and Paul

The only thing that I can think of that is harder than forgiving the people who have hurt you is forgiving yourself. It's much easier for me to excuse other people's mistakes than it is for me to excuse my own. I guess it's true what they say; you are your own biggest critic. Even now as I write this I wonder who will want to read religious advice from a rebel like me. Then... I am reminded of Peter.

I've always loved Peter and have found plenty of ways to relate to him. Peter was always that guy who let his mouth get him in trouble. He was known for correcting Jesus, talking out of turn, being a smartass, being quick to fight, and many times being doubtful of whether or not Jesus really knew what he was talking about. One time Jesus even called him Satan![54] Yet, out of the twelve disciples, Jesus chose him to be one of his inner three, his closest friend.

---

[54] Matthew 16:23

I often wondered why it was that Jesus chose to do that. I mean, Peter, had to be a handful always mouthing off or correcting Jesus like he knew better. Still, Jesus held him close as one of His dearest friends and invited him to be one of the founders of His church.

I'm Peter. I let my mouth run without thinking, I let my sailor tongue wag without censorship, I correct God all the time somehow thinking I know how to handle things better. I'm sure I would have been the one to declare my unyielding loyalty to Jesus and then, a few hours later, run away with my tail between my legs in his darkest hour.

What is encouraging to me is the fact that Jesus really loves people like me and Peter! He holds us close and calls us out to be leaders in his revolution. Where others see a hot head Jesus sees passion and excitement at change.

Right after Peter denied Jesus 3 times and the rooster crowed (randomly at 3am) the Bible says that Jesus turned and looked straight at Peter.[55] He looked at him not with anger or sadness or disappointment. He looked at him with love and forgiveness sparkling from the tears in his eyes. I know this because he looks at me that same way.

---

[55] Luke 22:61

Many times I have failed him and many more will come. Still, in every failure, he looks at me with eyes of understanding. Eyes that drive me to chase after him with all the power in my being. I can imagine that day when Peter heard from the women of Jesus's empty tomb, as he took off in full sprint to see for himself, that look replayed in his mind.

Later we see Peter stepping up as a leader of the early church starting with the day of Pentecost when he stood up and shared the message of Christ in every language.[56] Peter's passion and loyalty became his assets as he transformed into a man of grace. We even find him being concerned about offending people with what he's eating, something the old Peter wouldn't have thought twice about.[57] All this because Jesus saw the softness behind Peter's armor.

Equally as encouraging is the story of Paul, another founding father of the church of grace. Paul was at the top of the spiritual chain. He was from the right family, went to the best school, and was one of the top religious leaders of his day. He even persecuted those who followed Christ and taught the message of grace. He did all the right

---

[56] Acts 2:14
[57] Acts 10

things, all the things that he thought would earn him God's favor.

God called him out, not as a result of his actions, to become one of those who he had so passionately persecuted. He had a life changing encounter with Christ and walked away completely different. It must have been hard for Paul to walk into the services of those he had hunted and tell his story, but he did. Now he is known for who he became not for who he was. He is a hero of the faith![58]

Whether you are a Paul or a Peter, grace is for you. That is the wonderful thing about grace; it's all inclusive. The hot headed rebel and the religious law keeper both sit together as equals at the table of grace. No matter what you have done or what roads life has led you down, there is a place for you here.

God is not careful about who he calls to his revolution. Your past, failures, tattoos, sexual orientation, addictions, anger issues, messed up family, love of law, or dedication to justice won't keep you from grace. Nothing can separate you from the love of Christ. Forgive yourself because He has already forgiven you. You are already enough for him. Dare to take in grace and let it help you

---

[58] Acts 22:1-21

see yourself the way he does. Let it fill you with passion and drive you to be a leader in the revolution.

19

One Second Nail Polish

I'm a pretty passionate person, if I find something worth fighting for I will give all I have for that cause. This caused a new issue to arise as I began living in grace. The more I took in how much favor God has for me, the more I was filled with desire to give back to his revolution. I threw myself into multiple ministries, giving most of my time and all of my energy to be a part of something bigger than myself.

Service is a good thing especially when it comes from desire after taking in how loved you are by God, but it can lead you to busyness and then burnout if it becomes where you find your identity. My passionate personality had led me down that path in the past as I distracted myself with helping others heal while I fell apart.

It's interesting how we classify things as destructive habits and other things as just part of life.
I'd dare to say that addiction to alcohol and addiction of busyness are just as destructive. Honestly, busyness is almost worse! Alcohol addiction wrecks your body, may cause your marriage to fall apart, your friends to drift

away, your kids to lose touch, and your heart to be heavy with loneliness. However, busyness addiction causes the same destruction only it also leaves you confused and frustrated with others as you exclaim, "I'm doing everything I'm *supposed* to do!"

I see this happen so often in our churches. I've been guilty of it. We focus on the tasks we need to accomplish that we overlook the people who just need us to take a moment and listen to their hurt. We set our eyes on our mission and forget to take time to keep ourselves healthy.

It's so extremely common in our world today! We have instant access to information, phones that can do everything, and email that can let us work from anywhere. We even have nail polish (which I may or may not possess) that you can put on in one second! I'm not kidding. That is a real thing! I mean, I get it because the 30 seconds it takes me to do my nails is WAY too long! There is also this new social app (also which I may or may not use) called "Vine" that allows you to only share 6 second long video clips because that is, apparently, how long the human attention span lasts.

It's no wonder that Jesus would say, "Come to me you who are weary and I will give you rest."[59] Or why we are told to be still and know that He is God. We have to take time away from the hustle and bustle of our busy lives and even our service of Him to just rest.

This isn't just about sitting and ardently studying our Bibles, unless that is where you find rest, but rather to just be still. Just take a breath, lay back, and be held. It's hard, especially for people like me who always like to be doing something productive.

You may be amazed to find that the more you take moments to rest and be poured into by God, the easier it will become to pour into others without any thought of getting something back. You have to be able to rest so that you can create spaces of rest for those around you.

A great illustration of this is the story of Mary and Martha.

Jesus came to Mary and Martha's town and Martha invited Jesus over for dinner. Now, it's important to know something about Jewish culture here to really get what is going on. Jews had a social scale which determined how you were treated, and how much honor or shame was given to you. This was a HUGE deal to them and affected the entirety of their lives. Their identities were built in this. Jesus was a rabbi, and having a rabbi over for dinner

---

[59] Matthew 11:28

was a great honor. He was usually accompanied by not only his talmadim (disciples) but also those who wanted to be around and learn from him. So, this wasn't just Mary, Martha, and Jesus having a little get together.

In this story, Martha is in the kitchen, she is preparing food and getting things set up for this meal. Getting out the good china, making sure they have enough food and enough room for all those who would want to come see Jesus and eat with them. She is doing everything a good Jewish woman is supposed to do.

Mary, on the other hand, has completely forsaken her responsibilities. She has scandalously refused her duty, bringing shame on her and her family, and doesn't really seem to care too much. This leaves Martha alone and frustrated as she is not only doing everything right but also being shamed by her sister. It's not long before she makes her frustration known.

> "...so she came up to him and said, "Lord, don't you care that my sister has left me to do all the work alone? Tell her to help me."

That seems like a reasonable response right? I mean, Mary is about to enjoy this meal too, there's a lot to do and Jesus is visiting, Martha needs some help! Martha must be thinking, "Jesus, don't you see I'm doing what is right and Mary is being irresponsible?"

Jesus' response reveals to us his heart.

"But the Lord answered her, "Martha, Martha, you are worried and troubled about many things, but one thing is needed. Mary has chosen the best part; it will not be taken away from her."[60]

Now, let's think about this for a moment, was Martha doing something wrong by cooking dinner for Jesus? No, In fact she was doing everything that her religion and her culture told her was the right thing to do. What Jesus is trying to get Martha to see here is that she had gotten so focused on doing things that she was missing out on experiencing Him.

And how relatable is this, don't we do the exact same thing?

We want to do the right things, be the right influences, and lead people to Him. Sometimes we become so focused on these things that we never stop to

---

[60] Luke 10:48-32 (NET)

be still, to take Him in. Jesus longs for us to rest in Him, hang out with Him, and take in all that He pours out onto us. He doesn't want us to do things to earn His praise; we already have it, we just have to sit down with Him and take it in!

Did you know that Jesus is the only god who offers rest, right here, right now? True discipleship is the only "religion" that offers you freedom to just be still. Jesus wants us to have rest. If the things we are doing for Him are making us weary and heavy laden... maybe they aren't really for Him. Maybe we do these things because we think we have to. Maybe we do them because if we don't no one will. Maybe we just think like Martha must have, "Well, it's what I'm *supposed* to be doing!" and in that moment we become critical and demanding of others who we think aren't doing as much as we are. We think we are demanded of so we demand—that's how we work.

We live in a world of noise, distraction, and demands, it's no wonder that we go through life so exhausted. Even when we're alone we're not really in silence. We're on our phones, listening to music, reading, watching TV, but do we ever really just stop, be still, and be silent?

It's important for us to spend time in silence, in rest, just being with Jesus.

Interestingly enough this is the same Mary we read about earlier in Luke who comes to Jesus and cries at his feet, pouring expensive perfume on Him, and wiping it up with her hair. Jesus declares her forgiven and she walks away forever changed. The next time we see her it's here in the living room with Jesus, taking in all that she can from Him. Now that is what I call experiencing grace![61]

Mary's journey started far from anything even remotely related to grace and acceptance. She came searching for Jesus out of the totality of the brokenness she was so aware of. Our journeys should be nothing different, just simply desire for something better born from our brokenness.

---

[61] John 11:2; Luke 7:36-50

20
The Never Ending Story

The journey of grace never really ends, it just changes form as we take it in. Life presents us with different circumstances and struggles that give us the opportunity to see new ways to take in grace and give it out. We will always be continually growing and constantly learning.

Living in grace doesn't always make things easier; in fact, sometimes it makes things harder. The world outside the grace bubble is radically different. You can walk into churches, hear messages, encounter people, and hear prayers fueled and driven by fear, guilt, shame, and reminders of our failures. Those very people, so shackled to their religion that they can't even see the truth of Jesus, cut down the beacons of grace around them.

It's a battlefield out there. There is a very real war going on. Satan does not want the message of grace to get out, and he will try everything in his power to destroy it. It's so easy to get tunnel vision. It's easy to forget how hard it is living unshackled in a prison, offering the prisoners keys to their chains only to be met with rejection and lack of desire to be free.

There will be times when you feel discouraged. There will be times when you want to give up and run back to the person you were before. There will even be times when you feel unwanted, shackled, and broken.

In those times, take heart. Hold onto the hope that none of those things make you any less perfect before God. Remind yourself of who you are and take in the peace that he pours over you in every moment. He gently calls you loved when you feel unwanted. You are free even when you feel shackled. You are whole even when you seem broken.

My life has been a long and broken road. It has been filled with triumphs and failures, depths of depression and heights of joy. I have been a sinner and a saint. I don't know all the answers to all the theological questions that leaders in churches discuss; I don't have long passages of scripture memorized or pray long drawn out prayers. There is one thing I know, one thing that I am more confident in than anything else in my life, and that is grace.

I will fight for it. I will teach it. I will learn everything I can about it. It was the one thing that reached into my brokenness and offered me hope. While I was unable to do anything it gave me power. When I had lost who I was it brought me to life.

Rules can't do that. Law doesn't have that power. Structure, aggressive pushes towards conformity, even biblical knowledge, all lack that power. Nothing can do what grace can do.

I now see a God who is not just with us but who is for us. He fights for us, sacrifices for us, and gives into us. He created this planet for us and when we screwed that up He sent His son to die for us. He's not just this passive friend who tags along beside us; he is the brother in arms who joins our revolution! Even when we have a hard time having faith in Him, He has unwavering faith in us. He is jealous for us, not in anger and selfishness hoarding us away like some precious ring with mystic powers, but because He is in a passionate love relationship with us and longs for fellowship with us.

He longs for us to experience the oneness we have with Him. He is unpredictable in His blessings, excessive in his love, frustratingly inclusive in his grace, reckless in His mercy, and actively involved in our lives. I am increasingly grateful for a God who is patient in my stubbornness, love in my anger, peace in my anxiety, and calm in my restlessness. My God looks at me, sees all that I am, and says, "Rock on, baby!" That is what God looks like to me now.

I want people to experience that God. I want people to see how wonderful it is to be free. I want those outside the church to know that Jesus isn't that judgmental church goer, fire and brimstone pastor, look of disgust, or list of rules. That's not who he ever was. I want people inside the church who are held captive by law to know that there is something better out there. There is a way to be right with God that doesn't exhaust you at every moment. There is a way to find passion again. There is way to have life that is filled with peace and rest.

Whoever you are at the time you find yourself reading this, I hope you know above all else that you are loved. You are loved with a love that gives life to the dead, heals incurable illness, brings down evil kings, raises up simple farm boys, strengthens nations, and brings hope to individuals. You are loved for all that you are. You are loved in spite of where you've been. You are loved even if you don't measure up to people's expectations of you. You are loved.

I hope reading this book helps you experience some kind of freedom or at the very least makes you think a little deeper about how God sees you. I hope you question me, disagree with me, get frustrated, and go searching to see if I'm right. Then I hope you see grace, not as just a definition you learned in Sunday school, but as something worth giving everything else up for. I hope to see you join the revolution.

Special Thanks

Luanne Hays (Mom) - For being my editor, sounding board, and encourager. And for helping to open my mind and see things from the opposite perspective of my own.

Ms. Lynette Green- For being someone who taught me the importance of words and making me believe that writers have the power to change the world.

Phil Humbert- For being an incredible friend and for claiming the title of my life coach. You really had no idea what you were getting yourself into did you?

Brian Treadaway- For introducing me to radical grace and being patient with me as I went through religion detox.

Eli Da Silva and Steve Freeman- For being men of character and integrity, for teaching me what real leadership looks like, and for believing that my ministry is important.

Carolina Da Silva- For more reasons than I can fit on this page, but most of all for encouraging me to believe in impossible things and helping me achieve them.

Chance "Poo Pah" Hays- For always having faith in me, even when I didn't have faith in myself and for never letting me forget who I really am.

46602331R00106

Made in the USA
Lexington, KY
09 November 2015